A MIDSUMMER NIGHT'S DREAM

SHAKESPEARE FOR KIDS

JEANETTE VIGON

Copyright © 2023 Jeanette Vigon
All rights reserved.
ISBN: 9798878989794

This book is a modern adaptation for children of William Shakespeare's "A Midsummer Night's Dream," which is a work in the public domain. While the original story and characters are based on Shakespeare's play, this adaptation includes significant original content tailored for a young audience. These additions include simplified language and reimagined scenes, specifically created to make this timeless tale accessible and engaging for young readers. The intention of this adaptation is to introduce children to the classic story in a manner that respects the essence of Shakespeare's original work, while presenting it in a way that is relatable and understandable for a younger audience.

"We can say of Shakespeare, that never has a man turned so little knowledge to such great account."

— T. S. ELIOT

WHY I WROTE THIS BOOK THE WAY I DID

When I embarked on the journey of adapting Shakespeare's plays for children, my primary goal was to bridge the gap between the timeless allure of Shakespeare's narratives and the imaginative worlds of young readers. The decision to adapt these plays for children was driven by a desire to introduce them to the richness of literary classics at an early age, fostering a love for literature that could grow with them.

Choosing to maintain the original structure of acts and scenes was a deliberate effort to preserve the integrity and rhythm of Shakespeare's works. This approach not only honors the original compositions but also introduces young readers to the conventions of drama and the beauty of structured storytelling. It was important to me that children experience the plays as they were intended, albeit in a more accessible form.

Incorporating literary language while ensuring it remains engaging and understandable for children was a balancing act. I aimed to simplify the complexity of Shakespeare's language without diluting its power and beauty. By carefully selecting vocabulary and crafting sentences that convey the essence of the original plays, I aspired to captivate young minds and stimulate their intellectual curiosity.

Adapting these plays also involved making thoughtful choices about content, ensuring that themes and scenes were appropriate for a young audience. This required a sensitive approach to storytelling, where the lessons of love, loyalty, betrayal, and justice are presented in a manner that is both educational and entertaining.

In summary, the creation of this book was a labor of love, guided by the belief that Shakespeare's works are not just for adults but for everyone. By adapting these plays for children, I hope to plant the seeds of appreciation for classic literature in the fertile ground of young imaginations, encouraging a lifelong journey of reading, learning, and discovery.

I truly hope you will enjoy reading it, as much as I enjoyed re-writing it.

INTRODUCTION

Welcome to the enchanting and whimsical world of "A Midsummer Night's Dream," where we venture into the magical forests outside Athens, a realm where the ordinary meets the extraordinary. This isn't just any tale; it's a fantastical journey of love, mischief, and the spellbinding power of dreams.

Our story unfolds in an age where messages were sent with the speed of a fairy's flight, not through instant messages, and where a moonlit forest could be the stage for both comedy and romance. In this mystical setting, a diverse cast of characters finds themselves entangled in a web of enchantments and misadventures.

In one corner of the forest, we have the spirited lovers, caught in a tangle of affections that not even they can unravel. But this is no simple love story—it's a dance of

INTRODUCTION

desire and confusion, choreographed by the mischievous Puck and overseen by the fairy king and queen, Oberon and Titania, whose own quarrel sets the night alight with magic.

Fear not, for this journey through the woods is not all about love's complexities. We'll sprinkle our path with laughter and whimsy, courtesy of a band of hapless craftsmen preparing a play for the Duke of Athens. Their earnest but bumbling efforts will bring a smile to your face and remind you that art and heart can turn even the most far-fetched plot into a masterpiece.

So, gather your sense of adventure and prepare to be whisked away to "A Midsummer Night's Dream," where the boundary between dream and reality blurs. Imagine enchantments that turn folly into wisdom, forest chases that are more exhilarating than any video game, and a narrative that teaches us about the power of imagination, the beauty of nature, and the endless possibilities of love.

Are you ready? Then let's join the star-crossed lovers, the feuding fairies, the aspiring actors, and the ingenious Puck as we dive into a story that has delighted audiences for generations, now reimagined with a joyful and child-friendly twist. Here we go, into the spellbinding world of "A Midsummer Night's Dream," where every leaf whispers a story, and every star shines with a secret!

ACT 1

SCENE 1

In the bright halls of Athens, Theseus looked at Hippolyta with excitement. "My dear Hippolyta, our wedding is so close, just four days away! But this waiting feels so long, like time itself is crawling."

Hippolyta smiled gently, "Don't worry, Theseus. The four days will pass in the blink of an eye, and then we'll celebrate under the light of a new moon."

Theseus then turned to Philostrate, "Let's fill Athens with laughter and joy. I want no sadness at our wedding."

Philostrate nodded and left to do as asked. Theseus continued, "Hippolyta, I won your heart in battle, but our marriage will be a time of joy and celebration."

Just then, Egeus stormed in with his daughter Hermia and two young men, Lysander and Demetrius. "Greetings, Duke Theseus," Egeus began. "I'm here because my daughter refuses to marry Demetrius, who I've chosen for her. Instead, she's been charmed by Lysander."

Turning to face Lysander, Egeus accused, "You've stolen Hermia's heart with your poems and gifts, under the moonlight."

Lysander met his gaze, unafraid, while Hermia stood silently, her loyalty clear.

Egeus looked at Theseus, pleading, "According to our laws, if Hermia won't marry Demetrius, she faces grave choices. I ask for your judgment."

Theseus faced a difficult decision, caught between the law and the young lovers' wishes. The air was filled with tension, as everyone awaited his response.

Theseus, standing tall and authoritative, turned to Hermia with a serious tone, "Hermia, think carefully. Your father is like a god to you, shaping your life. Demetrius is a good man."

"But so is Lysander," Hermia quietly insisted.

"Theseus acknowledged, "True, Lysander is good, but without your father's approval, Demetrius is deemed more suitable."

Hermia's voice was soft yet determined, "I wish my father could see through my eyes."

"Theseus responded firmly, "But you must see through his eyes and judgment."

Hermia, with a hint of desperation, pleaded, "Please understand, I don't know what makes me brave enough to say this, but what's the worst that could happen if I don't marry Demetrius?"

Theseus laid out the harsh reality, "You must either face death or vow never to marry, living a nun's life, forever parting from the company of men."

Hermia's resolve was clear, "Then I'll accept that. I'd rather live and die this way than marry Demetrius against my will."

"Theseus advised her to take time to think, "By the next new moon, decide: obey your father, marry Demetrius, or live a single life dedicated to Diana."

Demetrius tried to persuade her, "Please, Hermia, and Lysander, give up your claim to her."

Lysander stood firm, "You have her father's blessing, let me have Hermia's love."

Egeus, ever stern, supported Demetrius, "Lysander, my love for Demetrius makes him the rightful choice. Hermia is mine, and I give my right to Demetrius."

Lysander argued back, "I am just as noble, as wealthy, and, more importantly, Hermia loves me. And don't forget, Demetrius, you once wooed Helena, who still loves you."

The room was tense, each person standing their ground, as the complex web of love and duty became ever more entangled.

After the tense discussion, Theseus admitted he had heard rumors about Demetrius's past actions and decided to take Demetrius and Egeus aside for a private talk. He warned

Hermia again to obey her father's wishes or face Athens's harsh laws.

Leaving with Hippolyta, Theseus tasked Demetrius and Egeus with a special assignment related to his wedding. Egeus gladly followed, eager to see his wishes fulfilled.

Once the elders left, Lysander turned to Hermia, noticing her sadness, "Why do you look so sad, my love?"

Hermia replied, "Perhaps it's because I've been crying so much."

Lysander sighed, "It seems true love always faces obstacles. Whether it's differences in family, age, or the approval of friends."

Hermia added, "Or even worse, when outside forces threaten to tear it apart."

Lysander then proposed a plan, "Listen, Hermia, I have an aunt who lives far from here. She treats me like her own son, and there, away from Athens, we can get married. If you really love me, meet me tomorrow night outside the town, in the woods where we once met with Helena."

Hermia, filled with hope, promised to meet him, "I swear by all that's sacred, I'll be there for you."

As they reaffirmed their promise, Helena arrived, adding to the complexity of their situation. Helena lamented how Demetrius loved Hermia's beauty and wished she could win his love with Hermia's charm.

Hermia shared her frustration with Helena, "Even when I'm unkind to him, he still loves me."

"Oh, if only your frowns could teach my smiles to attract such love!" Helena wished.

"I've even scolded him, yet he responds with love," Hermia said.

"How I wish my prayers would bring me such affection," sighed Helena.

"The more I try to push him away, the more he follows," Hermia explained.

"And the more I love him, the more he dislikes me," Helena lamented.

Hermia reassured her, "His actions are not my fault, Helena."

Helena envied, "If only I could be blamed for being beautiful!"

Hermia then confided in Helena about her plan to escape with Lysander, "Since meeting Lysander, Athens, which once seemed like paradise, now feels like a prison because of our love's troubles."

Lysander added, "Helena, we plan to escape Athens tomorrow night, under the cover of darkness, when the moon reflects on the world."

"And we'll meet in the woods, where you and I have shared many secrets," Hermia continued, inviting Helena's support for their plan and wishing her luck with Demetrius.

"Keep our secret, Lysander. We'll avoid each other until tomorrow night," Hermia concluded, signaling a temporary farewell.

After Hermia and Lysander left, Helena mused on the unfairness of love, "Some people are so lucky in love, while others, like me, are not. Even though I'm considered as beautiful as Hermia in Athens, Demetrius doesn't see me that way."

Reflecting on the nature of love, she noted, "Love doesn't see with the eyes but with the mind. That's why Cupid is blind, making choices without seeing clearly."

Determined, Helena decided to tell Demetrius about Hermia's plan, hoping it might bring her closer to him, despite the cost to her own heart.

SCENE 2

In the cozy home of Peter Quince, a group of eager craftsmen gathered, buzzing with anticipation for the play they were about to discuss, aimed to honor the Duke and Duchess on their wedding night.

Quince, looking around at the assembled friends, asked, "Is all our company here?"

Bottom, unable to contain his enthusiasm, suggested, "Best to call them one by one, as per the list, Peter Quince."

Quince, holding a scroll, announced, "This list names those chosen to perform in our play for the Duke and Duchess's wedding night."

Bottom, always keen to know more, urged, "Tell us about the play and then the roles, Peter Quince."

Quince revealed, "We're presenting 'The most

lamentable comedy, and most cruel death of Pyramus and Thisby.'"

"A fantastic choice, full of laughter and tears!" exclaimed Bottom. "Now, who will play which part?"

Quince began the casting, "Nick Bottom, the weaver, you're to play Pyramus."

Bottom, curious, inquired, "Pyramus, is he a lover or a tyrant?"

"A lover who bravely ends his life for love," Quince explained.

Bottom, brimming with confidence, declared, "I'll make the audience weep with me. Yet, I'd shine as a tyrant too, with grand speeches that could split the ears of the groundlings!"

He then performed a snippet of bombastic verse, showcasing his 'tyrant' persona, before urging Quince to continue with the cast list.

Turning to Francis Flute, Quince said, "You're up next, Flute, the bellows-mender."

"Here," Flute responded, stepping forward.

Quince assigned him, "You shall play Thisby, the lady loved by Pyramus."

Flute balked, "A lady? But I'm starting to grow a beard!"

Quince reassured him, "You can wear a mask and speak in a soft voice."

Unable to resist, Bottom interjected, "If I could hide my

face, I'd play Thisby too, speaking in a tiny voice for her lines!"

Quince, maintaining order, insisted, "No, Bottom, you are Pyramus. And Flute, you are Thisby."

With roles slowly being assigned amidst the laughter and playful banter, the group felt a growing excitement about bringing their unique talents to the grand occasion, each dreaming of the applause that awaited their heartfelt if unpolished, performance.

Robin Starveling stepped forward, "Here, Peter Quince."

"You'll be Thisby's mother," Quince assigned. "Tom Snout, the tinker."

"Here," Snout replied, ready for his role.

"Pyramus' father for you. I'll be Thisby's father. Snug, you'll take on the lion's part. I believe we have a complete cast now."

Snug, a bit worried, asked, "Is the lion's part written down? I'm not quick to learn."

Quince reassured him, "It's mainly roaring. You can manage that without a script."

Bottom, ever eager for more, boasted, "Let me play the lion! I can roar so well, it'll be a delight for the Duke!"

Quince, concerned, cautioned, "Too fierce a roar might scare the ladies, and we'd all be in trouble."

The group agreed, realizing the danger in frightening their audience.

Bottom, not deterred, claimed, "I can roar as gently as a dove or as sweetly as a nightingale."

Quince firmly replied, "No, Bottom, you're our Pyramus. He's the hero, handsome and charming, and that's the role for you."

Bottom then mused on the best beard for Pyramus, listing off various colors and styles.

Quince joked about Bottom playing "bare-faced" if he chose a French-crown-color beard, hinting at its baldness.

Quince then handed out the scripts, "Learn these by tomorrow night. We'll meet outside the town in the palace wood by moonlight to rehearse away from prying eyes. I'll also prepare a list of props we need."

Bottom rallied the group, "We'll rehearse thoroughly and boldly. Be perfect, adieu."

Quince set the meeting place, "At the duke's oak we meet."

Bottom concluded, "Enough said; let's prepare," and with that, they all departed, each to learn his part, excited and a little nervous about their secret rehearsal in the woods.

ACT II

SCENE I

In a shadowy wood near Athens, as the moon cast a soft glow through the trees, Puck, a mischievous spirit, encountered a Fairy flitting about.

Puck greeted the Fairy, "How now, spirit! Whither wander you?"

The Fairy, with a twinkle in her voice, replied, "Over hill, over dale, through bush, through brier, I wander everywhere, faster than the moon, serving the Fairy Queen. I sprinkle dew on her flowers and decorate each cowslip with pearls."

Puck, intrigued, warned, "The King holds his revels here tonight. Beware, lest the Queen come within his sight. Oberon's anger is fierce, all because the Queen has a lovely boy, a treasure she won't share with Oberon."

The Fairy recognized Puck, "Aren't you that tricky sprite,

Robin Goodfellow, known for causing mischief among the villagers?"

Puck proudly confessed, "Indeed, I am the merry wanderer of the night, always ready to make Oberon laugh with my tricks, like fooling a horse or tripping up an old gossip, turning laughter into music in the night."

As their banter continued, the atmosphere shifted with the arrival of Oberon and Titania, each with their own entourage, entering from opposite sides. The tension between them was palpable.

Oberon, with a touch of sarcasm, greeted Titania, "Ill met by moonlight, proud Titania."

Titania, undaunted, responded, "What, jealous Oberon! I've left your company and bed."

Oberon challenged her, "Stay, rash wanton. Am I not your lord?"

Titania countered, "And I your lady, yet I remember when you left our realm to whisper sweet nothings to a mortal woman. Why return now? Is it because the Amazon, Hippolyta, is marrying Theseus, and you wish to bless their union with joy?"

Oberon, with a mix of frustration and disbelief, addressed Titania, "How can you shame me about Hippolyta, when you yourself were entwined with Theseus's adventures? You led him through the night, away from those he wronged."

Titania, her voice cool and steady, responded, "Your

accusations are mere shadows of jealousy. Since the start of summer, we haven't met in joy. Your disputes have spoiled our celebrations, causing disturbances in the natural world. The seasons are confused, crops fail, and the mortal world suffers, all because of our discord."

Oberon, seeking to resolve their conflict, proposed, "Then mend these troubles. You have the power. I only ask for the boy to join my entourage."

Titania, with unwavering resolve, declared, "I will not barter the child with you. His mother was a follower of mine, and in her memory, I care for her son. I cannot betray her trust."

Oberon questioned her stay, to which Titania replied, "I plan to remain here until Theseus's wedding. Join our celebrations if you wish, but do not expect me to yield the boy."

With a sense of finality, Titania exited with her attendants, leaving Oberon to plot his revenge. He called for Puck, reminiscing about a magical moment with a mermaid that had the power to calm the sea, indicating he had a plan involving Puck's unique skills.

Oberon shared a memory with Puck, "I saw Cupid's arrow miss its intended target, quenched by the moon's beams. It struck a flower, turning it purple, a flower now with the power to make anyone fall in love with the first creature they see. Fetch me that flower, Puck."

Puck, eager to please, promised, "I'll circle the earth and have it to you in no time."

Once alone, Oberon plotted, "With this flower's juice, I'll make Titania fall in love with something vile. Then I'll bargain the boy from her in exchange for the antidote."

Hiding as Demetrius and Helena entered, Oberon listened. Demetrius was trying to shake off Helena, "Stop following me. I don't love you. I'm here for Hermia, not you."

Helena, undeterred, professed, "The more you reject me, the more I'll follow you. I love you like a faithful dog loves its master."

Demetrius, growing frustrated, warned, "Your persistence may turn my dislike into hatred."

Helena, hopelessly in love, responded, "I can't help but love you, even if it makes me sick."

Demetrius tried to reason with her about the impropriety of her following him, but Helena saw his presence as a beacon of safety, her love making her blind to the dangers of the forest.

Their conversation, filled with Helena's desperate pleas and Demetrius's cold rejections, painted a stark picture of unrequited love, setting the stage for Oberon's magical intervention.

Demetrius, in a huff, told Helena, "I'm going to run away from you and hide in the bushes, leaving you all alone for the wild animals to find."

Helena responded, not missing a beat, "Even the wildest animal isn't as mean as you. Go ahead and run; things will turn upside down: the hunter becomes the hunted, and the gentle ones chase the fierce."

Demetrius, trying to end the conversation, said, "Stop asking me to stay; let me go. And if you follow me into the woods, just know I might lead you into trouble."

Helena, undeterred and a bit upset, shot back, "Whether it's in the temple, the town, or the fields, you're always causing me trouble, Demetrius. It's not fair; we women can't fight for love the way men do. We're supposed to chase, not be chased." And with that, Demetrius stormed off.

Helena, with a determined look, said to herself, "I'll follow him anyway, turning this terrible situation into my own little heaven, just to be close to the one I love so much." And she too left.

Then Oberon, the fairy king, appeared, saying to himself, "Goodbye, young lady. Before he leaves this forest, he'll be the one chasing after you."

Puck, Oberon's helper, came back with a special flower. "Here it is," he announced.

"Great, give it to me," Oberon said excitedly. "I know a place where Titania, the queen of the fairies, sometimes sleeps, surrounded by beautiful flowers and scents. I'll use this flower's juice to play a little trick on her, making her fall in love with the first thing she sees."

He then gave Puck another task, "There's a young woman from Athens, in love with a man who doesn't care for her. Use the flower on him, so he'll fall in love with her instead.

But make sure she's the first person he sees when he wakes up. You'll recognize him by his Athenian clothes. Do it carefully, so he ends up loving her more than she loves him. And meet me before dawn."

Puck, ever the loyal servant, replied, "Don't worry, my lord, I'll take care of it." And off they went, into the night.

SCENE 2

In another part of the forest, Queen Titania and her fairy friends were preparing for bedtime. "Let's dance and sing a little song," Titania suggested. "After that, you all have tasks to do: some of you will take care of the rosebuds, others will battle the bats for their wings to make coats for my little elves, and some will shoo away the loud owl that gets surprised by us every night. Sing me to sleep, then off you go to your duties."

The fairies sang a gentle lullaby to keep away any creatures that might disturb their queen. They sang of spotted snakes, thorny hedgehogs, and other creatures of the night, asking them to stay away from Titania. Their song was sweet and calming, filled with wishes for her safety and a peaceful rest.

After their song, the fairies left, and Titania fell asleep.

Oberon, the fairy king, saw his chance. He quietly approached and put some magical juice on Titania's eyelids. "The first thing you see when you wake up, you'll fall deeply in love with, no matter what it is," he whispered, hoping his plan would work.

Meanwhile, Lysander and Hermia, two young lovers, entered the same part of the forest. They were tired and lost. "My love, you look so tired," Lysander said to Hermia. "Let's rest here for the night and wait for daylight."

Hermia agreed, "Yes, Lysander. You find a place to sleep, and I'll rest here on this grassy bank."

Lysander, full of love, suggested, "Let's share this spot. One pillow for both of us, united in love and loyalty."

But Hermia, wanting to keep things proper, said, "No, dear Lysander, for my sake, stay a little further away. It's not right for us to be so close together before we're married."

Lysander tried to reassure her, "Oh, please understand, my intentions are pure. Our hearts are joined, so it's like we're already one. But if it makes you feel better, I'll stay over here."

Hermia felt a bit embarrassed but stuck to her decision for them to sleep apart, emphasizing the importance of modesty and respect. "Good night, Lysander. Let's keep our love strong and pure," she said, settling down for the night, each keeping a respectful distance from the other.

Lysander agreed with Hermia's prayer for loyalty, wishing for eternal love. "Amen to your beautiful wish," he said. "My life should end if my loyalty ever does. This will be my bed. May sleep bring you all the rest you need!"

Hermia, touched by his words, replied, "I hope your wishes bring you just as much peace!" And with that, they both fell asleep under the starry sky.

As they slept, Puck, the mischievous fairy, wandered into their area. He had been searching all over the forest for an Athenian to use the love flower on, as Oberon had instructed him, but hadn't found anyone until now. "Who's this?" Puck whispered to himself, noticing Lysander's Athenian clothes. "This must be the man Oberon spoke of, the one who doesn't love the Athenian girl. And there she is, sleeping on the ground, not wanting to be too close to him. How respectful."

Without a second thought, Puck used the magic flower on Lysander, saying, "Now, when you wake up, the first thing you see, you'll fall head over heels for. Let love keep you awake." Satisfied with his work, Puck left to report back to Oberon.

Shortly after, Demetrius and Helena burst into the scene, with Helena pleading for Demetrius to stay. But Demetrius, annoyed and uninterested, told her to leave him alone and ran off.

Helena, exhausted and frustrated from the chase, lamented her unrequited love for Demetrius and envied Hermia's beauty, believing it to be the reason for Demetrius's affection towards Hermia instead of her. "How lucky Hermia is, with her bright, lovely eyes," she sighed. "I must look as frightening as a bear since animals run from me. No wonder Demetrius runs away from me as if I were a monster."

Then, she spotted Lysander on the ground and feared the worst. "Lysander, are you okay?" she asked, waking him.

Lysander, under the spell of the love flower, immediately professed his love for Helena. "I would walk through fire for you, Helena. Your beauty shines through, showing me your true heart," he declared, suddenly indifferent to Hermia and hostile towards Demetrius for Helena's sake.

Helena, confused and thinking Lysander was mocking her, tried to remind him of Hermia's love for him. "Why do you speak like this? Hermia loves you; you should be happy with that," she said, not understanding the sudden change in his affections.

Lysander, caught in the spell's magic, passionately told Helena, "No, I'm not happy with Hermia anymore. I regret every moment I spent with her. It's you I love, Helena. Why would I choose a raven when I could have a dove? My heart and mind are clear; you are the one I should be with. Your eyes are like chapters from the greatest love story."

Helena, feeling hurt and confused, responded, "Why are you being so cruel? Do you enjoy making fun of me? Isn't it enough that Demetrius doesn't want me, and now you mock my pain too? I thought you were kind, Lysander. It's so unfair that one man's rejection leads to another's mockery."

With those words, Helena stormed off, leaving Lysander to muse on his newfound disdain for Hermia. "Goodbye,

Hermia," he said, as if she could hear him. "May you never come near me again. My feelings for you have turned from sweet to sour, just like too much of a good thing can make you sick. And now, all my love and efforts will go towards winning Helena."

After Lysander left, Hermia suddenly woke up, terrified by a nightmare. "Lysander, help me!" she cried out, scared. "I dreamt a snake was eating my heart, and you just watched! Where are you, Lysander? Can you hear me?" But there was no answer, only silence. Feeling alone and desperate, she said, "If you're out there, please answer me. I'm so scared. If I can't find you, I might as well face death."

Determined to find Lysander or confront her fears alone, Hermia ran into the dark forest, calling out his name.

ACT III

SCENE 1

In a cozy spot in the woods, with Titania still asleep nearby, Quince and his troupe of amateur actors, including Bottom, Snug, Flute, Snout, and Starveling, gathered to rehearse their play.

"Are we all here?" Bottom asked, eager to start.

Quince confirmed, "Yes, and this is the perfect spot for our rehearsal. We'll use this green area as our stage and that thicket as our dressing room. Let's practice as we'll perform for the duke."

Bottom, always full of ideas, raised a concern. "There's a problem with our play, Pyramus and Thisby. Pyramus kills himself with a sword, and that might scare the ladies. What do we do about that?"

Snout and Starveling agreed it was a serious issue, with

Starveling noting that they might have to skip the killing scene altogether.

But Bottom had a solution. "No need to worry. We'll write a prologue to explain that no real harm will be done with the swords and that I, playing Pyramus, am not really Pyramus but Bottom the weaver. That'll calm their fears."

Quince agreed to Bottom's plan, deciding the prologue would be written in a specific poetic meter.

Then Snout brought up another concern. "What about the lion? Won't the ladies be scared of that?"

Bottom acknowledged the challenge. "Indeed, bringing a lion onstage could frighten the ladies. We need to make it clear that the lion isn't real."

He suggested that the actor playing the lion, Snug, should partially show his face and reassure the audience in a speech that he's actually a man, not a real lion, and introduce himself as Snug the joiner.

Quince agreed to this approach, but then they faced another dilemma: how to depict moonlight inside a chamber, since their story required Pyramus and Thisby to meet by moonlight.

After checking an almanac, they found that the moon would indeed shine on the night of their performance. Bottom suggested leaving a window open for the moonlight to enter or having someone represent Moonshine with a lantern and a bush of thorns.

Lastly, they discussed how to include a wall in their play,

as Pyramus and Thisby talk through a crack in a wall. Bottom proposed that an actor could play the Wall, using plaster, loam, or rough-cast to represent the wall and use his fingers to create a space for Pyramus and Thisby to whisper through.

With their creative solutions, the actors prepared to rehearse, working around their play's peculiar challenges with enthusiasm and a dash of inventive comedy.

Quince, eager to get the rehearsal underway, gathered his troupe. "Let's get settled, everyone. Pyramus, you're up first. After your speech, hide in that thicket, and everyone else follow your cues."

Just then, Puck snuck in, amused by the sight. "What do we have here? Some village folks putting on a play? This I have to see. Maybe I'll join in on their fun."

Quince, oblivious to Puck's presence, directed, "Pyramus, start us off. Thisby, get ready."

Bottom, with gusto, began, "Thisby, the flowers of odious savours sweet—"

"Odours, odours," Quince corrected gently.

"Right," Bottom continued, "odours savours sweet. So is thy breath, my dearest Thisby dear. But wait, I hear a voice! Stay here for a moment, and I'll be right back." He exited, leaving his fellow actors waiting.

Puck chuckled, "Never have I seen such a Pyramus."

Flute, looking around confused, asked, "Is it my turn now?"

"Yes, it's your turn," Quince confirmed. "Pyramus is just pretending to check on a noise. He'll be back."

Flute, as Thisby, then declared, "Most radiant Pyramus, most lily-white of hue, as true as the truest horse that would never tire, I'll meet thee, Pyramus, at Ninny's tomb."

Quince corrected him, "It's 'Ninus' tomb,' and you've jumped ahead. Wait for your cue."

"Got it," Flute said, trying to remember, "As true as the truest horse, that yet would never tire."

Then, Puck re-entered, this time with Bottom, who now had the head of an ass, thanks to Puck's magic. Bottom, unaware of his altered appearance, continued, "If I were fair, Thisby, I'd be only yours."

The absurdity of the situation, with Bottom's new look and the actors' confused attempts at rehearsal, made for a peculiar scene in the quiet woods, mixing the mundane with the magical in unexpected ways.

Quince, seeing Bottom with an ass's head, cried out in terror, "O monstrous! O strange! We are haunted. Run for it, everyone!" And they all scattered in fear, leaving Bottom alone.

Puck, delighted with the chaos he'd caused, promised to keep the fun going, transforming into various creatures to chase and confuse the frightened actors even more.

Left alone, Bottom wondered why his friends ran away. "Is this a joke to scare me?" he thought. Unfazed, he decided to stay and sing, proving he wasn't afraid.

Snout came back, shocked at Bottom's transformation. "O Bottom, you've changed! What's that on your head?"

"What? Do you see something strange on me?" Bottom replied, not realizing he had an ass's head.

Then Quince returned, only to exclaim in astonishment at Bottom's new look, "Bless you, Bottom, you've turned into something else!" before running off again.

Convinced they were all playing a trick on him, Bottom decided not to let it bother him. "They're trying to make a fool of me, to scare me. But I'll stay right here and sing," he declared.

As he sang about birds, his voice woke Titania, the fairy queen, who had been enchanted to fall in love with the first thing she saw upon waking. To her, Bottom's singing was the sweetest music.

"What angel wakes me from my sleep?" Titania marveled, enchanted by Bottom. "Sing again, dear mortal. Your voice and appearance captivate me. I love you at first sight."

Bottom, confused by this attention, replied, "Madam, you have little reason to love me. And yet, it's strange that reason and love are so seldom friends these days. But I can play along with a joke when needed."

Titania, completely under the spell's influence, found herself irresistibly drawn to Bottom, despite his unusual appearance, a testament to the powerful magic at work in the enchanted forest.

Titania looked at Bottom with admiration and said, "You're as smart as you are handsome."

Bottom modestly replied, "Well, I wouldn't say that. But I do wish I was smart enough to find my way out of this forest."

Titania quickly told him, "Don't wish to leave the forest. You're going to stay here with me, whether you like it or not. I'm no ordinary fairy; I'm quite important, and the summer depends on me. And because I love you, you'll come with me. I'll have fairies take care of you. They'll bring you treasures and sing you to sleep on a bed of flowers. I'll even make you so light and carefree, you'll feel like a fairy yourself."

Then she called her fairies, "Peaseblossom! Cobweb! Moth! Mustardseed!"

The fairies appeared, all saying, "Ready!" and asking, "Where shall we go?"

Titania instructed them, "Be nice to this gentleman. Play in his sight, feed him sweet fruits, steal honey for him, and use glow-worms to light his way at night. Use butterfly wings to fan him as he sleeps. Show him all the kindness you can."

The fairies greeted Bottom warmly, "Hail, mortal!"

Curious, Bottom asked, "What's your name?"

"I'm Cobweb," replied the fairy.

"Ah, Master Cobweb, I might need you if I get a cut. And who are you?" Bottom turned to another.

"Peaseblossom," came the answer.

"Please say hello to your parents for me, Master Peaseblossom. And your name?" he asked the next.

"Mustardseed," said the fairy.

"Ah, Master Mustardseed, I've heard of your family's bravery. I'd like to get to know you better too," Bottom said.

Titania then announced it was time to go to her bower. "The moon looks sad tonight, as if she's crying for love lost. Let's go quietly," she said, leading Bottom and the fairies away to pamper him in her magical home.

SCENE 2

Oberon, waiting in the woods, pondered aloud, "I wonder if Titania has woken up and whom she has fallen in love with first."

Just then, Puck arrived, and Oberon greeted him eagerly, "How goes the night, my merry spirit? What chaos reigns in this enchanted grove?"

Puck replied with glee, "Oh, it's a marvelous sight! The queen has fallen head over heels for a monster. A group of simple workmen were here, practicing a play in her sacred grove. The one playing Pyramus took a break, and that's when I saw my chance. I fixed a donkey's head on him, and when he returned, his friends scattered in terror, leaving him alone. And at that very moment, Titania woke up and instantly fell in love with him, donkey head and all."

Oberon couldn't help but laugh, "This is even better than

I had hoped for. But tell me, did you use the love potion on the Athenian man as I asked?"

Puck nodded, "Yes, I found him sleeping next to a woman. I used the potion, so she'd be the first thing he saw when he woke up."

As they spoke, Hermia and Demetrius walked into their midst. Oberon whispered, "Stay quiet, this is the Athenian woman."

Puck observed them and realized his mistake, "That's the lady, but this isn't the man I enchanted."

Demetrius, looking at Hermia, pleaded, "Why do you speak so harshly to me, when all I have is love for you? Why treat me like your worst enemy?"

Hermia, upset and worried, confronted Demetrius, "I'm angry with you, but I have a feeling you've done something far worse. If you've harmed Lysander in his sleep, you might as well drown me too because I can't live without him. Lysander was as faithful as the sun; he would never leave me while I slept. It must be that you've killed him; you look just as guilty and terrible as a murderer should."

Demetrius, hurt by her accusations, replied, "If I look guilty, it's only because your harsh words have pierced me. Yet, despite your accusations, you shine as brightly as Venus in the night sky."

Hermia, desperate for answers, pressed on, "Stop changing the subject. Where is Lysander? If you care about me at all, tell me where he is."

Demetrius, with a cold heart, retorted, "I'd rather feed him to my dogs."

Hermia, outraged, called him a monster, "You're beyond cruel! If you've killed him, you're no longer worthy to be called a man. Did you kill him in his sleep? That's the act of a coward, not a man."

Demetrius tried to calm her, "You're letting your anger cloud your judgment. I haven't killed Lysander; I have no idea where he is."

Hermia, still not satisfied, demanded, "Then at least tell me he's alive."

Demetrius, feeling trapped by the conversation, wondered, "And what would I gain from telling you that?"

Hermia declared, "The only thing you'll gain is never having to see me again. Goodbye, whether Lysander is alive or not." And with that, she stormed off.

Demetrius, knowing he couldn't chase after her in her current state, decided to stay put. "Her anger is too fierce to follow. I'll stay here and rest, weighed down by sorrow and loss."

As he lay down to sleep, Oberon observed the scene and realized Puck's mistake. "What have you done? You've caused confusion among two who truly loved each other, turning true love into chaos instead of fixing a mistaken love."

Oberon, seeing the mess created by Puck's mistake, decided to take matters into his own hands. "Go quickly, find

Helena of Athens. She's sick with love, looking pale and sighing for love's pain. Use your magic to bring her here. I will prepare a charm for Demetrius's eyes so that he will fall in love with her as soon as he sees her."

Puck, eager to rectify his mistake, replied, "I'm on it! I'll be back before you know it," and darted off like an arrow.

Oberon then prepared a special charm, using a flower hit by Cupid's arrow. "Let this potion make Demetrius love Helena as soon as he wakes and sees her, shining as bright as Venus in the sky."

Puck quickly returned, announcing Helena's approach and mentioning that Lysander, whom Puck had mistakenly enchanted, was with her, pleading for her love. "Shall we watch their foolish attempts at love? Mortals can be so entertaining with their mistakes."

Oberon suggested they hide, as the commotion might wake Demetrius. "Let's see how this unfolds with two men chasing one woman. I always find joy in these human follies."

As Lysander and Helena entered, Lysander was earnestly trying to convince Helena of his love, bewildered by her accusations of mockery. "Why do you think I'm mocking you? My tears and vows are genuine."

Helena, frustrated and confused by the sudden shift in affections, accused Lysander of playing cruel games. "Your promises are empty, just like the vows you made to Hermia. How can you dismiss her so easily for me?"

Lysander insisted his love for Hermia was a mistake, claiming his true affection was for Helena. "Demetrius loves Hermia; he doesn't care for you."

At that moment, Demetrius woke up, having been enchanted by Oberon's potion, and immediately professed his undying love for Helena, using extravagant comparisons to praise her beauty. "Oh, Helena, you are more divine than any comparison. Your eyes outshine crystals, your lips are tempting cherries, and your skin is purer than snow."

The enchanted declarations from both men put Helena in an even more incredulous and distressed state, as the scene turned into a tangled web of misplaced affections and magical interventions.

Helena, feeling deeply hurt and betrayed, accused Lysander and Demetrius of cruelly mocking her for their amusement. "It's cruel to play with someone's feelings just for fun," she lamented, believing their sudden declarations of love were just a mean-spirited game.

Lysander tried to clarify the situation to Demetrius, insisting that he was genuinely giving up his claim on Hermia in favor of Helena, whom he now loved. "I'm sincere in my love for Helena and renounce any claim to Hermia," he declared, hoping to resolve the conflict.

Helena dismissed their words as mere mockery, unable to believe that their affections could change so quickly and drastically.

Demetrius, affected by Oberon's enchantment, firmly

stated his love for Helena had returned, stronger than ever, and that he no longer had any affection for Hermia. "My heart is truly Helena's now," he affirmed, hoping to convince her of his sincerity.

As the argument heated up, Hermia re-entered, confused and concerned by the sounds of the dispute she overheard. She questioned why Lysander had left her alone, using the darkness of the night as a metaphor for her confusion and pain at his absence.

Lysander, now under the spell's influence, cruelly suggested that his love for Helena was the reason he left Hermia, causing Hermia to question the sincerity of his love. "How could you abandon me for Helena?" she asked, bewildered and heartbroken by his harsh words.

The scene became increasingly complicated as true feelings and magical enchantments clashed, leaving each person confused and hurt by the others' actions and words. The once clear relationships were now tangled in a web of jealousy, love, and misunderstanding.

Helena, feeling utterly betrayed, accused Hermia of joining the men in a cruel joke against her. "You're all working together to make fun of me," she cried, hurt by what she saw as a betrayal of their deep, lifelong friendship. Helena reminisced about their close bond, comparing it to two cherries on a single stem, inseparable and identical in their affection and interests.

Hermia, genuinely confused, responded, "I'm just as

shocked by your accusations. I haven't scorned you; it seems like you think I have."

Helena continued, questioning why Lysander and Demetrius, who were both in love with Hermia, were now professing their love for her, suggesting that Hermia must have encouraged them. "Why are they suddenly adoring me, the one they used to ignore, if not to mock me at your behest?"

Hermia was bewildered, unable to grasp the sudden shift in their affections and Helena's accusation. "I don't understand what you're talking about," she stated, confused by the entire situation.

Helena, heartbroken and feeling isolated, warned them to continue their cruel jest when she wasn't around. Despite feeling wronged, she blamed herself for the situation, suggesting that either her death or her departure would solve the problem, a statement reflecting her deep despair over the tangled emotions and loyalties at play.

Lysander stood firm, his eyes locked on Helena. "Please, Helena, listen to me: you are everything to me, my love, my everything!"

Helena couldn't help but smile, "Wow, that's so sweet!"

But Hermia, feeling upset, said, "Please, don't be mean to her."

Demetrius chimed in, "If she won't listen, I'll make her."

Lysander quickly responded, "You can't force anyone to

do anything. Your scary words are as weak as her gentle pleas. Helena, I truly love you, I swear it."

Demetrius insisted, "I love you more than he does."

Lysander challenged, "If you really think so, prove it!"

Demetrius was ready to act, "Let's go then!"

Hermia, confused and concerned, asked, "Lysander, why all this drama?"

Lysander, in his frustration, insulted her, which shocked everyone.

Demetrius suggested they pretend to chase him but not really follow, calling Lysander weak.

Lysander, getting angrier, lashed out at everyone, wanting them to leave him alone.

Hermia couldn't believe the harsh words, "Why are you being so mean? What's happened to you?"

Lysander, his anger boiling over, continued to insult Hermia and told her he didn't love her anymore.

Hermia was heartbroken, "Are you joking?"

Helena thought they were both playing a trick on her.

Lysander assured Demetrius he was serious, while Demetrius doubted Lysander's sincerity.

Lysander wondered aloud if harming Hermia would prove his point, but he knew he couldn't hurt her, even though he claimed to hate her.

Hermia was devastated, "Do you really hate me? Why? Wasn't I the one you loved just yesterday?"

Lysander coldly confirmed, "Yes, and I wish I never have

to see you again. Believe me, I truly hate you now and love Helena."

Hermia couldn't hide her shock and anger. "Oh, you trickster! You've stolen my love's heart like a thief in the night!"

Helena, feeling cornered, protested, "Really? Don't you have any shame? Why are you attacking me with such harsh words?"

Hermia, feeling insulted, shot back, "Puppet? Is that what you're calling me? So, you think you're better than me because you're taller?"

Helena tried to keep the peace, "Please, let's not fight. I never meant to upset you. I've always been your friend, Hermia. I only told Demetrius about your plan because I care for him, and now he's threatened me. I'll just go back to Athens and leave you all in peace."

Hermia, still fuming, said, "Well, then go! Who's stopping you?"

Helena replied sadly, "I'm leaving my foolish heart here."

Hermia snapped, "With Lysander?"

"No, with Demetrius," Helena corrected.

Lysander stepped in, "Don't worry, Helena. Hermia won't hurt you."

Demetrius agreed, "Yes, we won't let her hurt you, even if Lysander is trying to protect you."

Helena, feeling overwhelmed, exclaimed, "Oh, when

Hermia gets angry, she's really sharp and mean! She may be small, but oh, she's mighty fierce."

Hermia, feeling hurt by the repeated jabs about her size, protested, "Small again? Why do you let her make fun of me? I want to talk to her!"

Lysander, trying to insult Hermia back, called her a dwarf and a tiny, insignificant thing.

Demetrius warned Lysander, "You're too eager to help someone who doesn't want your help. Leave Helena out of this; if you show her any kindness, you'll regret it."

Lysander, feeling defiant, said, "Well, she doesn't care about me anymore. Let's see who Helena really prefers."

Demetrius agreed, "Fine, let's settle this once and for all," and they both left to confront each other.

Hermia, frustrated with Helena, said, "All this trouble is because of you!"

Helena, wanting to escape the conflict, replied, "I don't trust you and I don't want to be around you anymore. I might not be as quick to fight, but I can run fast to get away from this mess." And with that, Helena ran away.

Hermia, left alone, was stunned and speechless.

Oberon, watching from afar, criticized the mess, suggesting someone wasn't doing their job right or was causing trouble on purpose.

Puck, with a twinkle in his eye, spoke to Oberon, "My king, I must confess I was confused. You said the man would be in Athenian clothes, and that's who I thought I found. But, oh, how this mix-up has turned into quite the game!"

Oberon, observing the chaos among the lovers, had a plan. "Puck, it's time to thicken the night. Cover the sky with fog as dark as the underworld, and lead Lysander and Demetrius away from each other. Mimic their voices, provoke them, but ensure they don't actually meet. Once they're weary, make them sleep and use the special herb on Lysander's eyes to clear his vision. When they awake, all this trouble will seem like nothing but a dream, and they'll return to Athens in love and peace."

Puck nodded, understanding the urgency. "The night flies swiftly, and dawn is near. We must act quickly to avoid the light and keep our plans hidden from the day."

Oberon, confident in their fairy abilities, replied, "We have the power to roam and play until the dawn paints the sea golden. Yet, we must be swift. Let's fix this mess before the day begins."

With a mission in mind, Puck set off, chanting playfully, "Up and down, I'll lead them on a merry chase. I am feared in both field and town. Goblin, lead them up and down."

Soon, Lysander appeared, calling out into the night, "Where are you, Demetrius? Show yourself!"

Puck, seizing the opportunity for mischief, responded with a taunt, pretending to be Demetrius, "I'm here, ready for you. Where are you hiding?"

Lysander, fueled by determination, responded to Puck's taunting, "I'll catch up with you soon."

"Then follow me to clearer ground," Puck tricked him, leading him away. Lysander, thinking he was following Demetrius, exited, chasing the voice he heard.

Soon after, Demetrius entered, calling out for Lysander in frustration, "Lysander, where are you? Have you run away, you coward? Are you hiding?"

Puck, seizing another chance for mischief, called out to Demetrius, mocking him, "Are you boasting to the night, scared to face a real challenge? Come on, you coward, I'll teach you a lesson!"

Demetrius, thinking Lysander was taunting him, shouted back, "Are you there? Show yourself!"

"Follow my voice; we won't fight here," Puck led Demetrius away, continuing the game of chase.

Meanwhile, Lysander, tired and confused by the elusive voice, complained, "He keeps leading me on but disappears whenever I get close. I can't keep up with him. I'll rest here until daylight; then I'll find Demetrius and settle this."

Lysander, exhausted, lay down and fell asleep, hoping for daylight to aid his quest for revenge.

Not long after, Puck and Demetrius re-entered. Puck, with a laugh, taunted, "Ho, ho, ho! Why don't you come out, coward?"

Demetrius, frustrated and eager to confront his opponent, declared, "Face me if you dare! You keep running and hiding, never brave enough to face me. Where are you now?"

Puck, still up to his tricks, called out, "Come over here; I'm right here."

Demetrius, tired and frustrated, retorted, "You're just making fun of me. You'll regret this if I ever see you when the sun's up. I need to rest now." Overcome by exhaustion, Demetrius lay down, hinting at a confrontation come daylight, and quickly fell asleep.

Helena then re-entered, her voice weary with the night's events. "Oh, what a long night this has been. I wish the morning would hurry up so I can leave this place and the people who don't want me around." With that wish, she too found a spot to rest and closed her eyes to escape her loneliness.

Not long after, Hermia stumbled in, exhausted and disheveled. "I've never felt so tired or so sad. I'm all wet with dew and scratched by thorns. I can't walk another step. I hope Lysander is safe if there's a fight." With nowhere else to turn, she lay down, hoping for rest and the safety of her love.

Puck, watching the scene unfold, realized his work wasn't done. "So, we have three asleep. Ah, here comes the fourth. What a mess Cupid has made, turning love into such chaos."

With all four lovers now asleep, Puck got to work on fixing his mistake. Gently approaching Lysander, he said softly, "Now to correct the error I've made. This magic juice will make everything right." He applied the antidote to Lysander's eyes, murmuring, "When you wake, your heart will see clearly again. You'll love Hermia as you did before, and all this confusion will seem like a distant dream."

Puck, satisfied with his night's work, whispered a hopeful, "Now, every man will have his true love, and peace will return. Jack shall have Jill, and nothing shall go wrong. The man shall have his love back, and all shall be well." With that, he vanished into the night, leaving the lovers to find their way back to each other with the dawn.

ACT IV

SCENE 1

In the magical forest, Lysander, Demetrius, Helena, and Hermia were fast asleep. Titania, the queen of the fairies, and Bottom, who had a funny donkey's head instead of his own, entered the scene, followed by Peaseblossom, Cobweb, Moth, Mustardseed, and other fairy attendants, with Oberon, the king of the fairies, hiding and watching everything unseen.

Titania smiled at Bottom and said, "Come, sit down on this flower-covered bed. I'll gently touch your lovely cheeks, decorate your smooth hair with roses, and give your big, beautiful ears a kiss, my sweet joy."

Bottom looked around and asked, "Where's Peaseblossom?"

Peaseblossom popped up, "Here I am!"

"Please scratch my head, Peaseblossom. And where's Mr. Cobweb?" Bottom continued.

Cobweb appeared, "At your service."

"Mr. Cobweb, brave sir, grab your weapons, find a bee on a thistle for me, and bring back its honey. Just be careful not to break the honeybag; we wouldn't want honey everywhere. And where's Mr. Mustardseed?" Bottom asked, curious about his next fairy helper.

Mustardseed also showed up, "Ready for orders!"

"Thanks, Mr. Mustardseed. Just here to lend a hand to Mr. Cobweb with the scratching. My face feels so itchy with all this hair, I feel like I need a shave!" Bottom explained, finding the sensation amusing yet slightly annoying.

Titania, wanting to please Bottom, asked, "Would you like to listen to some music, my love?"

"I do enjoy music," Bottom replied, intrigued by the offer. "Let's hear some tunes made with tongs and bones."

"And what would you like to eat, my dear?" Titania continued, eager to cater to Bottom's every whim.

Bottom, feeling quite at ease in the magical company, shared his simple wishes, "I'd really like some food for horses, like a big bite of your best dry oats. And oh, a bundle of hay would be lovely. There's nothing quite like good, sweet hay."

Titania, ever so caring and wanting to please, replied, "I'll send one of my daring fairies to find the squirrel's stash and bring you fresh nuts."

But Bottom, with simpler tastes, said, "I'd prefer just a handful or two of dried peas. But please, let me be. I feel a strong need to sleep coming over me."

"Then sleep, and I'll hold you in my arms," Titania said lovingly, as she asked the other fairies to leave them be. And with that, they both fell asleep, wrapped in an embrace as natural as the vines entwining in the forest.

As they slept, Puck entered the scene, and Oberon, who had been watching, approached him, pleased with the sight.

"Welcome, Robin. Look at this tender scene," Oberon began. "I've begun to feel sorry for Titania's foolishness. After arguing with her for seeking the company of this silly man, enchanted to look like a donkey, I convinced her to give me the changeling boy she had taken. Now that I have what I wanted, I plan to fix her eyes and remove the donkey's head from this man."

Oberon, now feeling a bit of remorse, decided to undo the enchantments. "Be as you once were, see as you once did," he chanted, breaking the spell over Titania and planning to remove Bottom's donkey head so that when he and the others wake, they'll think of their experiences as nothing more than a strange dream.

"Now, my Titania, awake, my sweet queen," Oberon softly called, ready to restore everything to how it was meant to be, filled with love and regret for the chaos that had unfolded.

Titania, waking up from her strange dream, exclaimed in

surprise to Oberon, "My Oberon! I had the oddest dream! I thought I fell in love with a donkey."

Oberon pointed out, "There lies your so-called love."

Titania, now seeing clearly, wondered, "How did all this happen? Oh, I can't stand the sight of him now!"

Oberon called for quiet and instructed Puck, "Robin, please remove the donkey head from him. Titania, let's have some music to deepen their sleep even more."

Titania called for music, the kind that enchants sleep, as the music played softly in the background.

Puck, ensuring the enchantment's end, said, "When you wake up, you'll see with your own eyes again."

Oberon wanted the music to continue, "Let's join hands, my queen, and gently dance around these sleepers. Now that we're friends again, we'll celebrate with Duke Theseus tomorrow night, blessing his house and the marriages of the loving couples in joy."

Puck warned them, "My king, listen, I hear the morning bird singing."

Oberon, acknowledging the coming dawn, suggested, "Then, quietly let's follow the night's shadow. We can circle the earth faster than the moon travels."

Titania agreed, "Let's fly, my lord, and as we do, tell me how I ended up here, asleep among these mortals."

And with that, they exited, leaving the scene in tranquility.

Soon after, Theseus, Hippolyta, Egeus, and their

entourage arrived, ready to celebrate the day. Theseus sent someone to find the forester, eager to enjoy the hunt's music with Hippolyta. They planned to ascend the mountain and delight in the hounds' harmonious baying, echoing through the valleys, marking a joyful beginning to the day's festivities.

Hippolyta shared a memory with Theseus, "I once was with Hercules and Cadmus, hunting a bear in a Cretan forest with Spartan hounds. The sound of their barking was so powerful, it felt like the trees, skies, and waters joined in. I've never heard such a wild, beautiful noise."

Theseus proudly responded, "My hounds come from that same Spartan lineage, known for their majestic ears and strong build, slow in the chase but harmonious like bells when they bark. You've never heard a sound as melodious as theirs, not in Crete, Sparta, or Thessaly. You'll see what I mean soon."

But then, spotting the young Athenians asleep, he wondered aloud about their presence.

Egeus recognized them, "My lord, here lies my daughter Hermia, and with her are Lysander, Demetrius, and Helena. I'm puzzled to find them all together here."

"These young ones must have risen early to celebrate May Day, and hearing our plans, came to honor our ceremony," Theseus reasoned. "But Egeus, isn't today the day Hermia must make her choice?"

"It is, indeed," Egeus confirmed.

"Theseus suggested, "Let's have the huntsmen wake them with their horns."

As the horns sounded, Lysander, Demetrius, Helena, and Hermia woke up, startled.

"Good morning, friends. Valentine's Day is over, are you just now starting your romances?" Theseus teased.

Lysander, confused, apologized, "Forgive me, my lord."

"I'd like you all to stand," Theseus said. "You two were rivals. How is it that you're now here together, peacefully?"

Lysander tried to explain, still dazed, "My lord, I'm as confused as you are. I'm not fully awake yet and can't say for sure how we ended up here. But I think Hermia and I came here to escape Athens, to avoid the laws that threatened us."

Egeus, still upset, insisted, "Enough, my lord. I demand the law be enforced on Lysander. He tried to take Hermia away, defeating both you and me – you of your new wife and me of my consent for her to marry Demetrius."

Demetrius then spoke, "My lord, it was Helena who told me of their plan to escape to this forest. I followed them in anger, with Helena chasing after me. But somehow, my lord, my feelings for Hermia have vanished, like snow in the sun. Now, all my love is for Helena. I was promised to her before I ever met Hermia, but I had lost my taste for Helena as if I were sick. Now, it's as if I've recovered, and I truly love Helena and only her."

Theseus, seeing the situation unfold, said, "We've come upon a happy resolution. Egeus, I'll make the final decision.

In the temple soon, we will have a celebration where these couples will join in marriage. Since the day has grown late, we'll postpone our hunt. Let's return to Athens to prepare for a grand feast."

And with that, Theseus, Hippolyta, Egeus, and their company left for Athens.

Demetrius reflected on the strange turn of events, feeling as though everything was blurry and confusing.

Hermia added, "It's as if I'm seeing everything in a strange, doubled way, where everything seems uncertain."

Helena, feeling both amazed and bewildered, said, "It feels that way to me too. Demetrius is like a treasure I've found, both mine and not mine at the same time."

Demetrius, unsure of their reality, asked, "Are we truly awake? It feels like we might still be dreaming. Didn't the duke come here and ask us to follow him to the temple?"

"Yes, and my father was with him," Hermia added.

"And Hippolyta too," said Helena.

Lysander confirmed, "He did ask us to follow him to the temple."

Convinced by this, Demetrius suggested, "Then we must be awake. Let's follow him, and along the way, we can share what we dreamt about."

With that, they all exited, leaving the forest to follow Theseus's command.

Suddenly, Bottom woke up alone, "When it's time for my part, call me, and I'll be ready. 'Most fair Pyramus.' Oh, where is everyone? Peter Quince! Flute! Snout! Starveling! It seems they've left me here asleep. I've had the strangest dream, too bizarre for words. To try to explain it would make anyone seem foolish. It felt so real, yet indescribable. No one could understand or imagine what I've dreamt. I think I'll ask Peter Quince to write a song about my dream, calling it 'Bottom's Dream' because it's so deep and without end. I'll perform it at the end of our play for the duke. Maybe, to add to its charm, I'll sing it in memory of someone special."

With a plan in mind, Bottom left to find his friends and share the incredible adventure of his dream, ready to turn it into art.

SCENE 2

Back in Athens, at Quince's house, Quince and his friends, Flute, Snout, and Starveling, were worried.

"Has anyone checked on Bottom? Is he back yet?" Quince asked.

Starveling replied, "We can't find him anywhere. He must have been taken away by magic."

Flute was concerned, "If he doesn't show up, our play can't go on, right?"

Quince agreed, "It's impossible without him. No one else in Athens can play Pyramus as well as he can."

Flute added, "He's the smartest and most talented craftsman we have."

"And he's the best looking for the part, with a voice just perfect for Pyramus," Quince noted.

Flute corrected him, "You mean 'paragon.' A 'paramour' is something entirely different."

Just then, Snug arrived with news, "Everyone, the duke is on his way back from the temple, and more than one couple got married. If we had performed our play, we would have been set for life."

Flute sighed, "Oh, poor Bottom! He's missing out on earning money. He would have earned sixpence a day for life if the duke had seen him play Pyramus."

As they lamented, Bottom suddenly appeared, "Friends, where are you? What's happening?"

Quince exclaimed, "Bottom! You're back! What a wonderful surprise!"

Bottom declared, "I've got an amazing story, but I can't tell you everything now. Just know the duke has seen our play. Let's get ready quickly. Make sure your costumes are in order, put new ribbons on your shoes, and make sure Thisbe's costume is clean. The person playing the lion shouldn't cut his nails; they need to look like claws. And remember, no onions or garlic—we need to smell nice. They're going to love our play. No time to waste, let's go!"

With that, they all hurried off to prepare, excited and hopeful about their performance at the palace.

ACT V

SCENE 1

In the grand palace of Athens, King Theseus, Queen Hippolyta, and their friends were talking about a most unusual tale.

Hippolyta, with a hint of wonder in her voice, mentioned, "It's quite odd, Theseus, the story these young lovers have shared."

Theseus, shaking his head with a smile, replied, "Odder than fiction, I'd say. I can hardly believe such old tales and fairy stories. Those in love or touched by madness see the world in ways beyond what calm thought can grasp. They imagine things that aren't there, turning the air into stories and giving names to the invisible."

Hippolyta considered this, adding, "Yet, the adventures they recounted from last night, and how their feelings changed so completely, seems to prove there's more to it than mere fancy."

Just then, the four happy lovers, Lysander, Demetrius, Hermia, and Helena, arrived, their faces glowing with joy.

Theseus greeted them warmly, "Joy to you all and may love forever light your days!"

Lysander, full of happiness, wished the same for Theseus and Hippolyta.

Looking to fill the evening with entertainment, Theseus wondered, "What festivities can we enjoy tonight to pass the time before we retire? Where's the one who organizes our fun? Is there no play to soothe the waiting hours?"

With that, he called for Philostrate to arrange some merriment, setting the stage for an evening of joy and celebration.

Philostrate, the master of revels, approached King Theseus, ready to share the evening's entertainment options. He handed over a list for the king to choose from.

Theseus looked over the list, reading out loud the possible shows. "A battle with Centaurs, sung by a musician? No, we've celebrated that story before, in honor of Hercules."

He continued, "And what's this? A wild tale of Bacchanals in a frenzy? I've seen such things before. Not fitting for tonight."

Reading further, he found, "A play about the Muses mourning the loss of Learning? Too sharp and critical for a wedding celebration."

Then he came across something peculiar, "A short play about Pyramus and Thisbe, filled with both sadness and laughter? How strange, like mixing fire and ice!"

Philostrate explained, "Yes, my lord, it's a brief play, only about ten lines long, which might seem too long because it's so dull. There's not a single fitting word or actor in it. And though it ends in tragedy, with Pyramus taking his own life, the rehearsal brought us more laughter than tears."

This intrigued Theseus, the idea of a play so mixed in its emotions, offering a unique blend of entertainment for the evening.

Theseus turned to Philostrate, curious, "Who are the performers of this play?"

Philostrate replied, "They are hardworking men from Athens, my lord. This is their first attempt at such a task, and they've put much effort into memorizing their lines for your wedding."

Intrigued, Theseus declared, "Then we must see it."

Philostrate tried to dissuade him, "I fear it's not a play fit for your majesty. It's quite simple and possibly dull."

But Theseus was adamant, "Let's give them a chance. Nothing done out of simplicity and duty can be unwelcome. Bring them in."

As Philostrate left to fetch the performers, Hippolyta expressed her concern, "I'm not fond of watching efforts fail, especially when done out of duty."

"Theseus reassured her, "Dear, there's beauty in their attempt. We'll celebrate their effort, not just the execution."

Hippolyta, still unsure, mentioned, "Philostrate thinks they can't perform well."

To which Theseus smiled, "Then let's be all the more thankful for their effort. It's the intent that counts. In my travels, I've found warmth in the simplest greetings, even when they were awkwardly delivered. It's the heart behind the words that matters."

As Philostrate returned, he announced, "Your grace, the players are ready to begin their prologue."

Eagerly, Theseus and his guests prepared to watch the play, ready to find joy in the earnest efforts of the Athenian workmen, embracing the simplicity and sincerity of their performance.

As the trumpets sounded, Quince stepped forward to deliver the prologue. He explained, with earnest clumsiness, that their performance was meant to delight, not offend. Their intention was pure, hoping to showcase their humble talents.

Theseus commented lightly, "This speaker doesn't fuss over details."

Lysander added, "He delivered his introduction as awkwardly as a young horse learning to run. It's important not just to speak but to speak truthfully."

Hippolyta observed, "He handled his prologue as a child

does a new instrument—making sounds but without control."

"Theseus nodded, "His words were all jumbled up, like a knotted chain. Who's next?"

Then entered the actors for Pyramus and Thisbe, along with characters representing Wall, Moonshine, and Lion. The prologue continued, explaining each character's role in their tale of tragic love. Wall separated the lovers, Pyramus and Thisbe. Moonshine represented the light by which they planned to meet, and Lion was the beast that frightened Thisbe, leading to a tragic misunderstanding and the death of both lovers.

After the introduction of the characters, Theseus mused about the lion's role, wondering if it would speak.

Demetrius quipped, "In a play where many foolish things happen, why not a speaking lion?"

The anticipation grew among the audience, ready to see how this curious and earnestly presented tale would unfold, enjoying the simplicity and the heartfelt attempt of the performers.

Snout stepped forward, introducing himself as the wall that separated Pyramus and Thisbe. He explained, with a touch of pride, how he had a small hole through which the two lovers whispered their secrets.

Theseus, amused, joked, "Could anyone expect a wall made of mud and straw to speak any better?"

Demetrius laughed, "This must be the cleverest wall I've ever heard talk, my lord."

Then came Pyramus, portrayed by one of the workmen, lamenting the darkness of night and fearing that his beloved Thisbe had forgotten their meeting. He praised the wall for its role in their secret romance and desperately searched for the hole to glimpse his love.

"Thank you, kind wall," he said, "for letting me look through you. But alas, I can't see my Thisbe!"

Theseus couldn't help but comment, "It seems the wall should be upset for being called deceitful."

But Pyramus, staying in character, insisted, "No, that's for Thisbe to say when she arrives, and here she comes now."

Thisbe then appeared, expressing her own sorrow over their separation and her affection for the wall that, despite being a barrier, allowed them to communicate. She even spoke of kissing the wall's stones, which held them apart yet kept their love alive.

The audience watched, entertained by the earnest but comical performance, as the lovers praised and lamented their unusual intermediary.

Pyramus, with a hint of whimsy, declared, "I hear a voice! Now, I'll go to the crack in the wall to see if I can hear my Thisbe's face. Thisbe!"

Thisbe responded with affection, "My love, you are indeed my love, I believe."

Pyramus, ever the romantic, replied, "Believe what you

will, I am the grace of your love; steadfast like Limander."

"And I am faithful like Helen, until death do us part," Thisbe pledged in return.

Their exchange continued, comparing their loyalty to that of famous lovers of old. They even attempted a kiss through the wall's small gap, though they only managed to kiss the wall itself.

Pyramus then proposed, "Meet me at Ninny's tomb without delay?"

Thisbe agreed, "Through life or death, I will not delay."

After their vows, they exited, leaving the wall—Snout—to conclude his part with a bow, announcing his departure as the wall 'went away.'

Theseus mused on the wall's removal, symbolizing the end of the barrier between the lovers, while Demetrius joked about the wall's eagerness to participate in the story.

Hippolyta couldn't help but comment on the absurdity of the play, calling it the silliest she'd ever heard. Theseus, however, saw value in the power of imagination to transform even the simplest performance into something more significant.

Their discussion was interrupted by the entrance of Lion and Moonshine, ready to continue the play's fantastical journey. Lion, played by Snug the joiner, reassured the audience of his harmless nature, humorously clarifying he was not a real lion to prevent frightening them, setting the stage for the next act of this charmingly makeshift performance.

Theseus chuckled at the lion's introduction, "What a kind-hearted creature, with such a clear conscience."

Demetrius joined in the amusement, "Indeed, my lord, this is the finest portrayal of a beast I've ever seen."

Lysander added his own jest, "This lion has the courage of a fox!"

To which Theseus quipped, "Yes, but with the wisdom of a goose."

Demetrius playfully countered, "But, my lord, a fox is known for stealing geese, not for its bravery."

Theseus laughed, "Well, a goose wouldn't dare challenge a fox. Let's leave the lion to his act and turn our attention to the moon."

Moonshine then stepped forward, proclaiming, "This lantern represents the moon, and I am the man dwelling within it."

Demetrius couldn't resist a comment, "He should have worn the horns on his head to truly look the part."

Theseus observed, "But he doesn't resemble a crescent moon; you can't see any horns from here."

Moonshine repeated his explanation, attempting to clarify his role as the man in the moon, but Theseus pointed out the logical flaw, "The man should be inside the lantern, not beside it, to truly be the man in the moon."

Demetrius joked about the danger of getting too close to the candle inside the lantern, while Hippolyta expressed her weariness with the moon's lengthy explanation.

Theseus, trying to maintain a courteous atmosphere, suggested they allow Moonshine to complete his explanation despite the confusion.

Moonshine concluded simply, "I am here to tell you that the lantern is the moon, I am the man in the moon, this thorn-bush and this dog are mine."

Demetrius humorously noted that everything should be contained within the lantern if it truly represented the moon, emphasizing the playful scrutiny under which the performance was being watched.

As Thisbe entered, looking for her love near Ninny's tomb, the attention shifted back to the unfolding drama, momentarily pausing the banter among the spectators.

As the Lion roared on stage, Thisbe, played by one of the actors, ran off in fear.

"Well roared, Lion," Demetrius commended with a chuckle.

Theseus, amused by the scene, added, "And well run, Thisbe."

Hippolyta, looking at Moonshine, said with a smile, "And well shone, Moon. The moon truly does shine with grace tonight."

After the Lion's act of shaking Thisbe's mantle and exiting, Theseus observed, "Well moused, Lion."

Lysander quipped, "And just like that, the lion is gone."

"And here comes Pyramus," Demetrius announced as Pyramus made his entrance.

Pyramus, with heartfelt drama, thanked the Moon for its bright beams, believing they would lead him to his true love, Thisbe. But upon finding the blood-stained mantle, he descended into despair, lamenting the cruel fate that befell his beloved.

"Theseus remarked, "Such passion, and the death of a dear friend, could indeed make a man look sad."

Hippolyta, touched by the performance, admitted, "I can't help but feel sorry for him."

Pyramus then cursed the nature for creating lions, blaming such a beast for the loss of his dear Thisbe. Overcome with grief, he dramatically took his own life, declaring his soul's departure to the sky and bidding the world farewell.

As Pyramus ended his tragic monologue with repeated cries of "die," Demetrius wittily noted, "No die, but an ace for him; he is but one," lightening the mood with a play on words, even as the stage was wrapped in the mock tragedy of Pyramus's death.

Lysander playfully said, "He's even less than an ace, because he's not here anymore."

Theseus, trying to lighten the mood, joked, "Maybe if we call a doctor, he could wake up and be a bit silly."

Hippolyta was curious, "Why did the moon leave before Thisbe came back? Won't she miss seeing her friend?"

Theseus reassured her, "Don't worry, she'll find him under the starlight. Look, here she comes to finish our story."

Hippolyta hoped Thisbe wouldn't be too sad for too long, saying, "I hope she keeps it short for Pyramus."

Demetrius thought about who did their part better, saying, "It's hard to say who was better; both did so well in their own way."

Lysander noticed Thisbe's quick discovery, "She's found him already with her kind eyes."

Demetrius hinted at what Thisbe might say, "And now she's going to tell us how she feels."

Thisbe found Pyramus and was very sad, "Are you sleeping, my love? Oh no, why won't you answer me? Wake up, please!"

She talked about how much she would miss him, "We won't get to see your bright eyes or your smile anymore. You were always so kind and funny. We all will miss you so much."

Then, feeling very sad, Thisbe decided she wanted to be with Pyramus in a dream, saying goodbye to everyone, "Goodbye, my friends. I'll be with Pyramus in my dreams."

Theseus commented on the end, "Now, it's up to the moon and the lion to say goodbye to our friends."

Demetrius added with a smile, "And don't forget the wall, it was part of their story too."

Everyone smiled, enjoying the play's adventure, knowing it was all make-believe, and clapped for the actors who worked so hard to tell their story.

Bottom stood up and cheerfully said, "Don't worry, the

wall that kept their fathers apart is now gone. Would you like to see a short dance or hear the ending words from us?"

Theseus replied, "No need for ending words, please. Your play was good as it is. No need to say sorry. If the person who wrote this had played Pyramus and pretended to hang himself, it would have been a very sad story. But it turned out well and was very entertaining. Let's see the dance instead, and skip the ending words."

Then, they all watched a dance.

After the dance, Theseus noticed it was very late, "It's midnight, time for lovers to go to bed. We've stayed up way too late tonight. This play kept us awake and entertained. Let's go to bed now. We will celebrate like this for two weeks with more fun and games."

After everyone left, Puck came out and said, "Now it's the time of night where the lion roars and the wolf howls at the moon. The tired farmer is asleep, and the dim lights are flickering. The owl is screeching, reminding those in sadness of their gloom. It's the hour when spirits roam freely outside, and we fairies run around, making merry in the dark, following our queen's command. We make sure this house is peaceful and no creature disturbs it. I've come to sweep the dust away and keep it clean."

Then Oberon and Titania, along with their fairy friends, entered.

Oberon announced, "Let's light up the house with a

gentle glow from the sleepy fire. All fairies, hop and skip lightly, and follow me in song and dance."

So, they all sang and danced lightly through the house, spreading joy and laughter.

Titania smiled and said, "Let's practice our song together. Make each word as beautiful as a bird's tune. Holding hands, with our fairy charm, we'll sing and make this place magical."

After their enchanting song and dance, Oberon declared, "Now, until morning comes, let's wander through this house. We'll bless the newlyweds' bed, ensuring their future children will be lucky and happy. This blessing will also ensure that all three couples will always love each other truly. No unfortunate marks or traits will affect their children. With the magic of morning dew, let every fairy spread out and bless each room with peace. The owner of this house will always be safe and happy. Let's go now; don't delay. We'll meet again at dawn."

After they all left, Puck stepped forward and said, "If our acting has upset you, just think of it this way: you were only dreaming while watching our play. This story, light and not meant to be serious, was just a dream. Please, don't be upset. If you forgive us, we'll make everything right. As I'm a truthful Puck, if we're lucky to avoid criticism, we'll quickly fix any mistakes. Or else, you can call me a liar. So, good night to everyone. If you consider us friends, show it by clapping, and I promise to make everything right."

THE END

THE MAGIC BEHIND "A MIDSUMMER NIGHT'S DREAM"

A **Royal Performance**: "A Midsummer Night's Dream" was first performed around 1596, and it's believed to have been written for a noble marriage. Imagine the play being performed in the grand halls of a castle, with flickering torches and an audience of lords and ladies, all dressed in their finest attire, laughing and clapping at the humorous antics on stage.

The Language of Flowers: Shakespeare uses flowers and plants in the play not just for their beauty, but to convey secret messages. For example, the love-in-idleness flower causes people to fall madly in love with the next creature they see. In Elizabethan times, flowers had symbolic meanings, and Shakespeare cleverly used this to enhance the magical atmosphere of his play.

Puck's Many Names: The mischievous fairy Puck also goes by the name Robin Goodfellow. Puck is a shape-shifter and a trickster, and his name in folklore means a mischievous demon or sprite. The character embodies the unpredictable nature of the fairy world and adds a playful complexity to the story.

The Moon's Role: The moon is mentioned more than twenty times throughout the play, symbolizing changeability, romance, and the passage of time. Shakespeare uses the moon to set the mood of various scenes, reflecting the phases of love and the transformation of characters. The constant references to the moon also tie back to the idea of a midsummer night, a time when magical things are said to happen under the moon's watchful gaze.

Influences on Pop Culture: "A Midsummer Night's Dream" has inspired countless adaptations in music, opera, ballet, and film. Its timeless themes of love, magic, and transformation resonate across cultures, making it a favorite source of inspiration for artists and creators around the world.

The Globe Theatre: Imagine watching "A Midsummer Night's Dream" at the famous Globe Theatre in London during Shakespeare's time. The open-air, circular theater would have been filled with people from all walks of life, from the groundlings standing in the pit to the nobility seated in the galleries, all marveling at the spectacle.

Athens and the Ancient World: Though set in and around the city of Athens, Shakespeare's play takes liberties with historical accuracy, blending elements of Greek mythology with English folklore. This mix creates a fantastical setting that transcends time and place, inviting audiences into a world where anything is possible.

The Seasons and the Play: "A Midsummer Night's Dream" cleverly incorporates the themes of the seasons, reflecting the natural cycles of growth, change, and renewal. The play's events unfold in a dreamlike summer night, symbolizing a time of magic, mystery, and merriment.

Shakespeare's Wordplay: Shakespeare loved to play with words, and this play is full of puns, jokes, and double meanings that would have delighted Elizabethan audiences. His clever use of language not only entertains but also adds depth to the characters and the story.

A Tapestry of Plots: The play weaves together several different stories: the quarrel between Oberon and Titania, the misadventures of the four young Athenian lovers, the transformation of Bottom, and the performance of the Mechanicals. This structure creates a rich and complex narrative that showcases Shakespeare's skill as a storyteller.

THE LIFE OF WILLIAM SHAKESPEARE

Step back in time with us as we discover the exciting life of **William Shakespeare**—a storyteller whose magnificent tales have been told and retold for hundreds of years. Fasten your seatbelts for some amazing facts about the Bard of Avon!

Birthday Mystery: Believe it or not, we don't know exactly when Shakespeare was born. Historians guess it was around April 23, 1564, but that's all because of the date of his baptism. How curious that such a famous person has a birthday shrouded in mystery!

School Days: Young Shakespeare attended the King's New School in his hometown, where he learned important subjects like Latin, Greek, history, and poetry—all without the gadgets and technology students have today.

Word Wizard: Shakespeare had a way with words, inventing over 1,700 of them! Imagine, every time you say "bedroom" or "excitement," you're using words that Shakespeare introduced to the English language.

Globe Trotter - But Not Really: The Globe Theatre is where Shakespeare's masterpieces were first performed—not a globe you can spin, but a large, round, open-air theater where audiences marveled under the sky.

Super-sized Works: Our dear Bard wrote 37 plays and 154 sonnets. That's a lot of storytelling! If you wrote a poem every week of the year, you'd still be short of Shakespeare's sonnet count.

Nicknamed "The Bard": Shakespeare is often referred to as "The Bard of Avon." 'Bard' means poet, and indeed, Shakespeare was a master poet from the town of Stratford-upon-Avon.

Lovey-Dovey Lines: Shakespeare's words about love are so beautiful that they are still read at weddings and shared between sweethearts today. And if you've heard the phrase "to be or not to be," you're quoting one of his most famous lines!

Queen for a Fan: Queen Elizabeth I loved the theater, and Shakespeare's plays were some of her most enjoyed performances. It was quite the honor for Shakespeare to entertain her majesty with his work.

Shakespeare's Secret Code: Some folks believe that Shakespeare tucked away secret codes within his plays—making each performance not just a show, but also a puzzle full of hidden meanings.

Goodnight, Sweet Prince: At age 52, in the year 1616, Shakespeare took his final bow. His presence may be missed, but his stories live on, continuing to inspire, entertain, and provoke thought across the globe.

So there you have it—a little peek into the life of the man who has kept us company through his words for over four centuries. Open the pages of his stories, and let William Shakespeare's plays transport you to a world where imagination knows no bounds. Happy reading!

ABOUT THE AUTHOR

Jeanette Vigon is a vibrant storyteller hailing from the sun-kissed beaches of California, where her Spanish heritage infuses her writing with a colorful zest for life. Born to Spanish immigrants who carried stories of their homeland across the ocean, Jeanette's childhood was rich with tales that sparked her imagination and sowed the seeds for her future in storytelling.

After completing her education with a focus on early childhood development, Jeanette dedicated herself to the noble profession of teaching. As a beloved primary school teacher, she spent years enlightening young minds in the classroom. Her magical ability to turn even the most mundane lesson into a memorable adventure earned her admiration from both her pupils and peers.

However, the call of the pen proved too strong for Jeanette to ignore. Diving headfirst into the world of literature, she transitioned from shaping minds with chalk to enchanting them with words as a full-time writer. Her intimate knowledge of children's learning styles, combined with her rich cultural roots, enables her to craft stories that are not only engaging but also educational.

Jeanette's writing is characterized by its empathy, humor, and a deep understanding of what captivates children's hearts and minds. Whether retelling a classic Shakespearean tale or penning an original story, her books are beloved for their ability to bridge cultural gaps and bring diverse experiences to the forefront of children's literature.

Now, with several acclaimed titles to her name, Jeanette continues to share her passion for enriching young lives through reading. When she's not lost in her latest manuscript, you can find her indulging in her love for travel, exploring new destinations, and collecting fresh inspirations for her next enchanting narrative.

It's hard for books to get noticed these days. Whether you liked this one or not, please consider writing a review, thanks!

Jeanette Vigon

SHAKESPEARE FOR KIDS - OTHER BOOKS IN THE SERIES

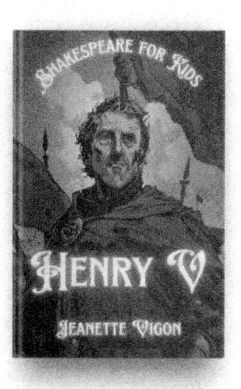

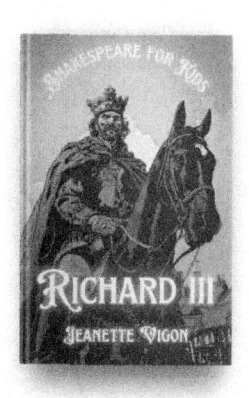

SHAKESPEARE FOR KIDS - OTHER BOOKS IN THE SERIES

SHAKESPEARE FOR KIDS - OTHER BOOKS IN THE SERIES

You can find the rest of the books in the series here:

https://amzn.to/3wLXpTC